Chemistry revision got you at boiling point?

AQA's 9-1 GCSE Chemistry exams can get pretty heated, but this CGP book is a great way to stay cool and composed throughout your revision.

It's packed with thirty quick tests covering every topic you need to know. Each one should only take ten minutes, so you won't need to block out hours of your life in one go. Just tackle them one at a time and you'll get there.

And finally, all the answers are included at the back of the book, so checking your work is a breeze! A cooling breeze, obviously.

CGP — still the best ☺

Our sole aim here at CGP is to produce the highest quality books
— carefully written, immaculately presented and
dangerously close to being funny.

Then we work our socks off to get them out to you
— at the cheapest possible prices.

Published by CGP

Editors:
Sharon Keeley-Holden, Charles Kitts, Dawn Wright

ISBN: 978 1 78294 845 2

With thanks to Alex Billings and Jamie Sinclair for the proofreading.
With thanks to Emily Smith for the copyright research.

Clipart from Corel®
Illustrations by: Sandy Gardner Artist, email sandy@sandygardner.co.uk
Printed by Elanders Ltd, Newcastle upon Tyne

Based on the classic CGP style created by Richard Parsons.

Text, design, layout and original illustrations © Coordination Group Publications Ltd. (CGP) 2017
All rights reserved.

Photocopying this book is not permitted, even if you have a CLA licence.
Extra copies are available from CGP with next day delivery • 0800 1712 712 • www.cgpbooks.co.uk

Contents

Topics for Paper 1

Test 1: Atomic Structure and the Periodic Table........2
Test 2: Atomic Structure and the Periodic Table........4
Test 3: Bonding, Structure and Properties..................6
Test 4: Bonding, Structure and Properties..................8
Test 5: Quantitative Chemistry...................................10
Test 6: Quantitative Chemistry...................................12
Test 7: Chemical Changes..14
Test 8: Chemical Changes..16
Test 9: Energy Changes..18
Test 10: Energy Changes..20

Mixed Tests for Paper 1

Test 11: Paper 1 Mixed Topics....................................22
Test 12: Paper 1 Mixed Topics....................................24
Test 13: Paper 1 Mixed Topics....................................26
Test 14: Paper 1 Mixed Topics....................................28
Test 15: Paper 1 Mixed Topics....................................30

Topics for Paper 2

Test 16: Rate and Extent of Chemical Change........32
Test 17: Rate and Extent of Chemical Change........34
Test 18: Organic Chemistry..36
Test 19: Organic Chemistry..38
Test 20: Chemical Analysis...40
Test 21: Chemical Analysis...42
Test 22: Chemistry of the Atmosphere......................44
Test 23: Chemistry of the Atmosphere......................46
Test 24: Using Resources...48
Test 25: Using Resources...50

Mixed Tests for Paper 2

Test 26: Paper 2 Mixed Topics....................................52
Test 27: Paper 2 Mixed Topics....................................54
Test 28: Paper 2 Mixed Topics....................................56
Test 29: Paper 2 Mixed Topics....................................58
Test 30: Paper 2 Mixed Topics....................................60

Answers..62

Progress Chart..67

Topics for Paper 1

Test 1: Atomic Structure and the Periodic Table

There are **12 questions** in this test. Give yourself **10 minutes** to answer them all.

1. True or False? "The further down Group 7 you go, the more reactive the elements get."

   A True

   B False

   [1]

2. When using fractional distillation to separate a mixture of liquids in the lab, which liquid will be collected first?

   A The liquid with the lowest boiling point.

   B The liquid with the highest boiling point.

   C The most abundant liquid.

   [1]

3. What is a substance made of only one kind of atom called?

   A An element

   B A compound

   C A metal

   [1]

4. True or False? "Chromatography can be used to separate out the different elements within a compound."

   A True

   B False

   [1]

5. Magnesium has 12 electrons. What will its electronic structure be?

   A 6, 6

   B 8, 4

   C 2, 8, 2

   [1]

6. True or False? "A group is a vertical column in the periodic table."

   A True

   B False

   [1]

7. True or False? "A mixture can only be separated into its parts by breaking the chemical bonds."

   A True

   B False

   [1]

8. True or False? "The number of protons in an atom is sometimes different to the number of neutrons."

   A True

   B False

   [1]

Topics for Paper 1: Atomic Structure and the Periodic Table

9. In the modern periodic table, what do the electronic structures of elements in the same group have in common?

   ....
   [1]

10. What are isotopes?

    ....

    ....
    [1]

11. Name the three different particles inside an atom and state the charge of each one.

    Particle: .... Charge: ....

    Particle: .... Charge: ....

    Particle: .... Charge: ....
    [3]

12. Why do Group 1 elements become more reactive as you go down the group?

    ....

    ....

    ....
    [2]

Test 2: Atomic Structure and the Periodic Table

There are **12 questions** in this test. Give yourself **10 minutes** to answer them all.

1. What is the name for the elements in Group 0 of the periodic table?

   A Alkali metals
   B Halogens
   C Noble gases
   [1]

2. What technique (or techniques) would be best for separating a mixture of salt and sand?

   A Evaporation
   B Filtration and crystallisation
   C Chromatography
   [1]

3. True or False? "Transition metals can form multiple types of ion."

   A True
   B False
   [1]

4. How did Niels Bohr suggest electrons were arranged in the atom?

   A Scattered within a ball of positive charge.
   B As a cloud surrounding the nucleus.
   C At fixed distances from the nucleus.
   [1]

5. Why were early versions of the periodic table incomplete?

   A The First World War broke out before they could be finished.
   B The Church forbade their completion.
   C Some elements had not been discovered yet.
   [1]

6. True or False? "Isotopes of the same element all have the same mass number."

   A True
   B False
   [1]

7. The first three elements of Group 7 are fluorine, chlorine and bromine. Which is the most reactive?

   A Bromine
   B Chlorine
   C Fluorine
   [1]

8. Which of the following is a typical physical property of non-metals?

   A Good conductor of electricity
   B Malleable
   C Dull looking
   [1]

Topics for Paper 1: Atomic Structure and the Periodic Table

9. State two things that are wrong in this diagram of the electronic structure of an atom.

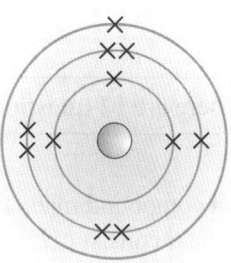

1. ....

2. ....
[2]

10. List three differences between the properties of a typical transition metal and those of a Group 1 metal. (You can ignore mercury for the purposes of this question.)

1. ....

2. ....

3. ....
[3]

11. Describe when a displacement reaction would occur between a halogen and a halide salt.

....

....
[1]

12. Balance the following chemical equation:

........Li + ...H₂O → ....LiOH + ...H₂
[1]

15

Test 3: Bonding, Structure and Properties

There are **12 questions** in this test. Give yourself **10 minutes** to answer them all.

1. What does a compound made up of a metal and a non-metal consist of?

    A Atoms

    B Molecules

    C Ions

    [1]

2. What type of structure does silicon dioxide have?

    A Giant covalent

    B Simple molecular

    C Ionic lattice

    [1]

3. True or False? "Pure metals are harder than alloys."

    A True

    B False

    [1]

4. Giant covalent structures have...

    A ...high melting points.

    B ...low melting points.

    [1]

5. What type of bond is formed when two hydrogen atoms form a molecule?

    A An ionic bond

    B A compound bond

    C A covalent bond

    [1]

6. In substances containing small molecules...

    A ...the intermolecular forces are much stronger than the covalent bonds within the molecules.

    B ...the covalent bonds within the molecules are much stronger than the intermolecular forces.

    C ...the covalent bonds within the molecules are the same strength as the intermolecular forces.

    [1]

7. True or False? "Ionic compounds conduct electricity when dissolved in water but not when molten."

    A True

    B False

    [1]

8. Which change of state does not take place at the boiling point of a substance?

    A Freezing

    B Condensing

    C Boiling

    [1]

Topics for Paper 1: Bonding, Structure and Properties

9. Describe the bonding in a Cl_2 molecule.

   ....

   ....

   ....
   [2]

10. Describe the structure of sodium chloride.

    ....

    ....

    ....
    [2]

11. Why are polymers usually solids at room temperature?

    ....

    ....
    [1]

12. Explain, in terms of its structure, why graphite conducts electricity.

    ....

    ....

    ....
    [2]

Test 4: Bonding, Structure and Properties

There are **12 questions** in this test. Give yourself **10 minutes** to answer them all.

1. Which of the following features is present in metallic bonding?

   A   Delocalised electrons

   B   A shared pair of electrons

   C   Two oppositely charged ions
   [1]

2. Why do ionic compounds have high boiling points?

   A   The bonds between the ions are weak.

   B   It takes a lot of energy to break the bonds between the ions.
   [1]

3. In which state of matter are the particles closest together?

   A   Gas

   B   Liquid

   C   Solid
   [1]

4. True or False? "Nanoparticles have a very low surface area to volume ratio."

   A   True

   B   False
   [1]

5. In the following example, what physical state is hydrochloric acid in?
   $Mg_{(s)} + 2HCl_{(aq)} \rightarrow MgCl_{2(aq)} + H_{2(g)}$

   A   Solid

   B   Gas

   C   Aqueous
   [1]

6. Which of the following best describes the structure of diamond?

   A   Sheets of carbon atoms arranged in hexagons

   B   Giant covalent structure

   C   Giant ionic lattice
   [1]

7. True or False? "Substances consisting of small molecules can conduct electricity."

   A   True

   B   False
   [1]

8. True or False? "A network of covalent bonds make graphene very strong."

   A   True

   B   False
   [1]

Topics for Paper 1: Bonding, Structure and Properties

9. Describe how ions are formed when a metal reacts with a non-metal.

....

....
[1]

10. Describe the structure of fullerenes. Give one example of their use.

....

....

....

....

....
[3]

11. Give two products that nanoparticles are used in.

1. ....

2. ....
[2]

12. Which of the substances in the table given below is a gas at 90 °C?

	Melting point (°C)	Boiling point (°C)
Ethanol	−114	78
Water	0	100
Iodine	114	184

....
[1]

Test 5: Quantitative Chemistry

There are **10 questions** in this test. Give yourself **10 minutes** to answer them all.

1. True or False? "Reactions with low atom economy are considered to be sustainable."

   A True
   B False
   [1]

2. True or False? "Percentage yield is calculated by dividing the maximum theoretical mass of product by the mass of product actually made and multiplying by 100."

   A True
   B False
   [1]

3. Grams per dm^3 is a measure of...

   A ...concentration.
   B ...mass.
   C ...volume.
   [1]

4. True or False? "In a chemical reaction, the mass of the products is always less than the mass of the reactants."

   A True
   B False
   [1]

5. True or False? "One mole of oxygen contains more molecules than one mole of hydrogen."

   A True
   B False
   [1]

6. How can you calculate the number of moles in a given mass?

   A Mass ÷ relative formula mass
   B Relative formula mass ÷ mass
   C Relative formula mass × mass
   [1]

7. In the following reaction equation, what number should come before HCl to balance the equation?
   $Zn + HCl \rightarrow ZnCl_2 + H_2$

   A 1
   B 2
   C 3
   [1]

8. A reactant that is completely used up in a reaction is called the...

   A ...excess reactant.
   B ...limited reactant.
   C ...limiting reactant.
   [1]

Topics for Paper 1: Quantitative Chemistry

9. Work out the mass of 2.5 mol of Mg(OH)$_2$.

Relative atomic masses (A_r): H = 1, O = 16, Mg = 24

....

....

....

.... g

[3]

10. A 25.0 cm^3 sample of potassium hydroxide (KOH) solution has a concentration of 0.200 mol/dm^3. This sample is completely neutralised by 40.0 cm^3 of sulfuric acid (H$_2$SO$_4$).

$$2KOH + H_2SO_4 \rightarrow K_2SO_4 + 2H_2O$$

Find the concentration of the sulfuric acid in mol/dm^3.

....

....

....

....

....

.... mol/dm^3

[4]

Test 6: Quantitative Chemistry

There are **11 questions** in this test. Give yourself **10 minutes** to answer them all.

1. What is the volume of one mole of oxygen at room temperature and pressure?

   A   24 dm^3

   B   24 cm^3

   C   24 mol/dm^3

   [1]

2. True or False? "During a chemical reaction no atoms are gained or lost."

   A   True

   B   False

   [1]

3. True or False? "The more solute there is in a given volume the less concentrated the solution is."

   A   True

   B   False

   [1]

4. What is the relative formula mass (M_r) of KOH?

   A   39

   B   28

   C   56

   [1]

5. What is the yield of a reaction?

   A   The mass of reactants used in a reaction.

   B   The temperature of a product.

   C   The amount of product obtained.

   [1]

6. When taking repeat readings of an experiment, what does a large range of results suggest?

   A   A small uncertainty in the results.

   B   A large uncertainty in the results.

   C   That the method used is accurate.

   [1]

7. When a metal reacts completely to form a metal oxide, the mass of the metal oxide formed will be...

   A   ...greater than the mass of the metal used.

   B   ...less than the mass of the metal used.

   C   ...the same as the mass of the metal used.

   [1]

8. What is the Avogadro constant?

   A   The number of particles in one mole of substance.

   B   The volume that one mole of gas occupies.

   C   The relative atomic masses of all the atoms in a molecule added together.

   [1]

Topics for Paper 1: Quantitative Chemistry

9. The theoretical yield of product X from a reaction is 50 g. The actual yield is 36 g. Calculate the percentage yield of product X.

....

Percentage yield = ... %
[2]

10. What is the concentration of the solution, in g/dm³, if 0.00025 kg of NaOH are dissolved in 0.5 dm³ of water?

....

....

....

.... g/dm³
[2]

11. Write a balanced symbol equation for the reaction when 280 g of iron reacts with 80 g of oxygen gas to give iron oxide.

Relative atomic masses (A_r): O = 16, Fe = 56

....

....

....

....

Symbol equation:..
[3]

Test 7: Chemical Changes

There are **12 questions** in this test. Give yourself **10 minutes** to answer them all.

1. What does a pH of 7 indicate?

   A   An acidic solution

   B   An alkaline solution

   C   A neutral solution
   [1]

2. True or False? "An insoluble base will react with an acid."

   A   True

   B   False
   [1]

3. True or False? "Hydrochloric acid and magnesium react to produce magnesium chloride and hydrogen."

   A   True

   B   False
   [1]

4. In electrolysis, at the negative electrode, positively charged ions...

   A   ...lose electrons.

   B   ...gain electrons.

   C   ...dissolve.
   [1]

5. An alkaline solution of potassium hydroxide reacts with nitric acid to produce...

   A   ...carbon dioxide and water.

   B   ...a metal oxide and water.

   C   ...a salt and water.
   [1]

6. What can you say about the pH of a carbonic acid solution compared to that of a sulfuric acid solution with the same concentration?

   A   It's the same

   B   It's lower

   C   It's higher
   [1]

7. Which process can be used to find the reacting volumes of acid and alkali solutions?

   A   Titration

   B   Distillation

   C   Electrolysis
   [1]

8. Which reaction shows the oxidation of iron?

   A $Zn + FeSO_4 \rightarrow ZnSO_4 + Fe$

   B $Fe + CuSO_4 \rightarrow FeSO_4 + Cu$

   C $2Fe_2O_3 + 3C \rightarrow 4Fe + 3CO_2$
   [1]

Topics for Paper 1: Chemical Changes

9. Name the two gases formed in the electrolysis of sodium chloride solution.

1. ....

2. ....
[2]

10. Give the ionic equation for the reaction between hydrogen ions and hydroxide ions during a neutralisation reaction. Include state symbols in your answer.

....
[1]

11. Electrolysis can be used to extract aluminium from a molten mixture of aluminium oxide and cryolite. Describe the reactions that occur at the electrodes during this process.

Negative electrode: ....

....

Positive electrode: ....

....
[2]

12. Why does the positive electrode need to be continually replaced during the electrolysis of aluminium oxide?

....

....
[2]

Topics for Paper 1: Chemical Changes

Test 8: Chemical Changes

There are **11 questions** in this test. Give yourself **10 minutes** to answer them all.

1. True or False? "All metals are found in the ground as ores."

   A True

   B False

   [1]

2. True or False? "Metals below carbon in the reactivity series can be extracted by reduction using carbon."

   A True

   B False

   [1]

3. Iron reacts with oxygen to form iron oxide. What kind of reaction is this?

   A Oxidation reaction

   B Reduction reaction

   C Neutralisation reaction

   [1]

4. How does the concentration of hydrogen ions change between pH 2 and pH 3?

   A It increases by a factor of 10.

   B It decreases by a factor of 10.

   C It increases by a factor of 1.5.

   [1]

5. Which is the correct ionic equation for the displacement of calcium ions by sodium?

   A $Na_{(s)} + Ca^{2+}_{(aq)} \rightarrow Na^+_{(aq)} + Ca_{(s)}$

   B $Na_{(s)} + Ca^{2+}_{(aq)} \rightarrow Na^{2+}_{(aq)} + Ca_{(s)}$

   C $2Na_{(s)} + Ca^{2+}_{(aq)} \rightarrow 2Na^+_{(aq)} + Ca_{(s)}$

   [1]

6. Which reactants can't you use to make magnesium sulfate?

   A Sulfuric acid and magnesium.

   B Sodium sulfate and magnesium.

   C Sulfuric acid and magnesium carbonate.

   [1]

7. True or False? "Hydroxide ions make solutions acidic."

   A True

   B False

   [1]

8. How can a solid salt be obtained from a salt solution?

   A By adding an indicator.

   B By adding a catalyst.

   C By crystallisation of the salt solution.

   [1]

Topics for Paper 1: Chemical Changes

9. Name the two products formed in the reaction between hydrochloric acid and copper oxide.

1. ....

2. ....
[2]

10. Name a metal that is extracted from its ore by electrolysis, and explain why it is extracted this way.

Metal: ....

Explanation: ....

....
[2]

11. Describe what you'd observe in the reactions of magnesium with dilute hydrochloric acid and iron with dilute hydrochloric acid. Give a reason for the difference between the two reactions.

....

....

....

....

....
[3]

Test 9: Energy Changes

There are **11 questions** in this test. Give yourself **10 minutes** to answer them all.

1. What is a battery?

   A A single cell.

   B Two or more cells connected in parallel.

   C Two or more cells connected in series.
   [1]

2. Which of these uses an endothermic reaction?

   A Hand warmer

   B Sports injury pack

   C Self heating drinks can
   [1]

3. True or False? "Hydrogen can be oxidised in a fuel cell."

   A True

   B False
   [1]

4. To break a chemical bond...

   A ...energy must be supplied.

   B ...energy must be released.
   [1]

5. In an endothermic reaction, the products are at...

   A ...a lower energy than the reactants.

   B ...a higher energy than the reactants.
   [1]

6. True or False? "A non-rechargeable cell contains chemicals which undergo reversible reactions to produce charge."

   A True

   B False
   [1]

7. What is the activation energy of a reaction?

   A The total energy of the reactants.

   B The minimum amount of energy needed by the particles to react.

   C The maximum amount of energy needed by the particles to react.
   [1]

8. Which of the following can be used to measure the energy change when a chemical reaction takes place?

   A Change in colour

   B Change in mass

   C Change in temperature
   [1]

Topics for Paper 1: Energy Changes

9. The equation below shows the combustion of methane.

$$CH_4 + 2O_2 \rightarrow CO_2 + 2H_2O$$

Here are the structures of methane, oxygen, carbon dioxide and water.

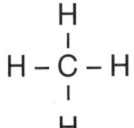   O = O   O = C = O   H—O—H (bent)

Using the bond energies below, work out the overall energy change for the combustion of methane:

C – H: 413 kJ/mol, O = O: 496 kJ/mol, C = O: 803 kJ/mol, O – H: 464 kJ/mol

....

....

....

....

.... kJ/mol
[3]

10. Give two advantages of using hydrogen fuel cells instead of batteries to power cars.

1. ....

2. ....
[2]

11. Does this energy level diagram show an exothermic or an endothermic reaction? Explain your answer.

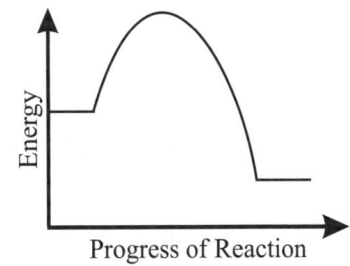

....

....
[2]

Test 10: Energy Changes

There are **11 questions** in this test. Give yourself **10 minutes** to answer them all.

1. In an endothermic reaction, the energy released when bonds are formed is...

   A   ...less than the energy used in breaking old bonds.

   B   ...greater than the energy used in breaking old bonds.
   [1]

2. A simple cell contains two different metals in contact with...

   A   ...an electrolyte.

   B   ...an electrode.

   C   ...hydrogen
   [1]

3. True or False? "Energy is conserved in all chemical reactions."

   A   True

   B   False
   [1]

4. True or False? "The reaction between hydrochloric acid and sodium hydroxide, an alkali, is exothermic."

   A   True

   B   False
   [1]

5. If the surroundings increase in temperature during a reaction...

   A   ...the reaction is endothermic.

   B   ...the reaction is exothermic.

   C   ...no new chemical bonds have formed.
   [1]

6. When an alkaline battery stops producing charge...

   A   ...it must be replaced, as it is non-rechargeable.

   B   ...it can be recharged by connecting it to an external electric current.
   [1]

7. Which equation shows the overall reaction in a hydrogen fuel cell?

   A   hydrogen + carbon dioxide → water

   B   hydrogen + oxygen → carbon dioxide

   C   hydrogen + oxygen → water
   [1]

8. If a reaction takes in energy from the surroundings, the products of the reaction have...

   A   ...more energy than the reactants.

   B   ...less energy than the reactants.

   C   ...equal energy to the reactants.
   [1]

Topics for Paper 1: Energy Changes

9. The equation for the formation of hydrogen chloride is: $H_2 + Cl_2 \rightarrow 2HCl$
   The overall energy change of this reaction is –184 kJ/mol.
   Sketch a reaction profile for this reaction and label the overall energy change.

   [3]

10. Give two examples of types of reaction that are exothermic.

    1. ....

    2. ....
    [2]

11. A student prepared three electrochemical cells. Each cell contained the same electrolyte and one electrode made of sodium. The second electrode in each cell was made from a different metal that is less reactive than sodium.

    The voltage produced by each cell is shown in the table below.

Cell	1	2	3
Voltage (V)	2.2	4.3	3.6

    In which cell is electrode B made from the most reactive metal? Explain your answer.

    ....

    ....

    ....

    ....
    [2]

Test 11: Paper 1 Mixed Topics

There are **11 questions** in this test. Give yourself **10 minutes** to answer them all.

1. True or False? "Atoms of the same element all have the same number of neutrons."

   A   True
   B   False
   [1]

2. When carbonates react with dilute acid they produce...

   A   ...carbon dioxide.
   B   ...hydrogen.
   C   ...oxygen.
   [1]

3. Which of the following would you expect to have the lowest boiling point?

   A   A giant ionic structure
   B   A substance containing small molecules
   C   A giant covalent structure
   [1]

4. How are the elements arranged in the modern periodic table?

   A   In order of atomic number.
   B   In order of atomic mass.
   C   In the order that they were discovered.
   [1]

5. What are metal oxides?

   A   Acids
   B   Salts
   C   Bases
   [1]

6. What is an exothermic reaction?

   A   A reaction which transfers energy to the surroundings.
   B   A reaction which takes in energy from the surroundings.
   [1]

7. True or False? "When forming an ionic bond, metal atoms lose electrons to form positive ions."

   A   True
   B   False
   [1]

8. What type of compounds are formed when alkali metals react with non-metals?

   A   Covalent compounds
   B   Ionic compounds
   [1]

9. Calculate the number of moles in 50 g of Na_2CO_3.
Give your answer to 3 significant figures.

Relative atomic masses (A_r): Na = 23, C = 12, O = 16

....

....

....

....

.... mol
[3]

10. State the two products formed in a reaction between a metal and an acid.

1. ....

2. ....
[2]

11. An element has the electronic structure 2, 8, 4.

Which group of the periodic table must it be in? Explain your answer.

....

....
[2]

Test 12: Paper 1 Mixed Topics

There are **11 questions** in this test. Give yourself **10 minutes** to answer them all.

1. How many molecules of CO_2 are in one mole?

   A   44

   B   1

   C 6.02×10^{23}

   [1]

2. In an exothermic reaction the energy required to break bonds is...

   A   ...less than the energy released when new bonds form.

   B   ...greater than the energy released when new bonds form.

   [1]

3. An element has a mass number of 23 and an atomic number of 11. How many neutrons does it have?

   A   11

   B   12

   C   23

   [1]

4. Halogen X will displace halogen Y from an aqueous solution of its salt if halogen X is...

   A   ...more reactive than halogen Y.

   B   ...less reactive than halogen Y.

   [1]

5. An ionic compound is made up of Na^+ ions and Br^- ions. What is its formula?

   A   NaBr

   B Na_2Br

   C $NaBr_2$

   [1]

6. True or False? "All covalent substances have a giant covalent structure."

   A   True

   B   False

   [1]

7. What is the mass of one mole of carbon?

   A   16 g

   B   6 g

   C   12 g

   [1]

8. Oxidation is...

   A   ...gain of electrons.

   B   ...loss of electrons.

   [1]

Mixed Tests for Paper 1

9. Explain why some batteries can be recharged but others cannot.

   ....

   ....

   ....

   .... [2]

10. What mass, in g, of carbon dioxide is formed when 120 dm³ of oxygen reacts with methane?
    The relative formula mass of CO_2 is 44.

    $$CH_{4(g)} + 2O_{2(g)} \rightarrow CO_{2(g)} + 2H_2O_{(g)}$$

    ....

    ....

    ....

    ....

    .... g
    [4]

11. Explain the difference between a strong acid and a weak acid in terms of ionisation.

    ....

    .... [1]

Test 13: Paper 1 Mixed Topics

There are **11 questions** in this test. Give yourself **10 minutes** to answer them all.

1. When a chemical bond forms...

   A ...energy must be supplied.

   B ...energy is released.

   [1]

2. True or False? "Atoms have no overall electric charge."

   A True

   B False

   [1]

3. Which of these is an endothermic reaction?

   A Combustion

   B Thermal decomposition

   C Neutralisation

   [1]

4. What is the pH scale used to measure?

   A The mass of a solution.

   B The temperature of a solution.

   C How acidic or alkaline a solution is.

   [1]

5. CH_4 and Cl_2 are...

   A ...simple molecules.

   B ...polymers.

   C ...giant covalent structures.

   [1]

6. What name is given to the total number of protons and neutrons in an atom?

   A Atomic mass

   B Atomic number

   C Mass number

   [1]

7. True or False? "Pure metals can be bent because the layers of atoms can slide over each other."

   A True

   B False

   [1]

8. Which of the following is an electrolyte?

   A A molten or dissolved ionic compound.

   B An electric current running through a solution.

   C A positively charged electrode.

   [1]

9. Describe the structure of an ionic compound. What holds the ions together?

....

....

....
[2]

10. A scientist wanted to use the following reaction to produce $MgCl_2$.
Calculate the atom economy of the reaction.

$$Mg + 2HCl \rightarrow MgCl_2 + H_2$$

Relative atomic masses (A_r): H = 1, Mg = 24, Cl = 35.5

....

....

....
[2]

11. 66 g of carbon are burnt completely in oxygen to produce CO_2.

The equation for the reaction is: $C + O_2 \rightarrow CO_2$.

Calculate the mass of CO_2 produced.

Relative atomic masses (A_r): C = 12, O = 16

....

....

....

....

.... g
[3]

15

Test 14: Paper 1 Mixed Topics

There are **11 questions** in this test. Give yourself **10 minutes** to answer them all.

1. The reaction inside a handwarmer is...

   A   ...endothermic

   B   ...exothermic
   [1]

2. True or False? "Nanoparticles have different properties compared with bulk amounts of the same material."

   A   True

   B   False
   [1]

3. When lithium reacts with water, the resulting solution is...

   A   ...acidic.

   B   ...alkaline.

   C   ...neutral.
   [1]

4. Beryllium is in Group 2 of the periodic table. What is the charge on a beryllium ion?

   A   2+

   B   1+

   C   2–
   [1]

5. What happens to the boiling points of the elements as you go down Group 0?

   A   They decrease

   B   They increase

   C   They remain constant
   [1]

6. Which of the following is an advantage of using the ball and stick model to represent a molecule?

   A   The gaps between the atoms in the molecule are accurately shown.

   B   The relative sizes of the atoms in the molecule are accurately shown.

   C   The arrangement of all the atoms is shown.
   [1]

7. True or False? "A solution with a pH of 1 is very acidic."

   A   True

   B   False
   [1]

8. Which of the following will not reduce the percentage yield of a reaction?

   A   Side reactions occurring.

   B   Starting with less reactants.

   C   A reversible reaction not going to completion.
   [1]

9. Describe how to carry out a titration to determine the volume of strong acid needed to neutralise a strong alkali.

   ....

   ....

   ....

   ....

   ....

   ....
   [4]

10. 1.84 g of ethanol (C_2H_5OH) is burnt completely in oxygen.
    Find the number of moles of carbon dioxide gas produced.

    $$C_2H_5OH + 3O_2 \rightarrow 2CO_2 + 3H_2O$$

    Relative formula mass (M_r) of C_2H_5OH = 46.

    ....

    ....

    .... mol
    [2]

11. Suggest one property of transition metal compounds that makes them suitable for use in paint.

    ....
    [1]

Test 15: Paper 1 Mixed Topics

There are **12 questions** in this test. Give yourself **10 minutes** to answer them all.

1. True or False? "Soluble salts can be made by reacting an acid with a carbonate."

   A True

   B False

   [1]

2. Which of these describes a metallic structure?

   A A giant structure of metal atoms held together by ionic bonds.

   B A giant structure of metal atoms arranged in an irregular pattern.

   C A giant structure of metal ions arranged in a regular pattern.

   [1]

3. True or False? "Smaller molecules have higher melting and boiling points than larger molecules."

   A True

   B False

   [1]

4. Metal atoms react to form...

   A ...negative ions.

   B ...positive ions.

   C ...covalent molecules.

   [1]

5. The discovery of the electron led to the...

   A ...plum pudding atomic model.

   B ...Bohr atomic model.

   C ...modern nuclear atomic model.

   [1]

6. True or False? "In an electrochemical cell, the smaller the difference in reactivity of the electrodes, the bigger the voltage of the cell."

   A True

   B False

   [1]

7. The reaction of citric acid and sodium hydrogencarbonate is...

   A ...endothermic.

   B ...exothermic.

   [1]

8. For environmental reasons it is better to use reactions with...

   A ...a low atom economy.

   B ...a high atom economy.

   [1]

9. A sodium hydroxide solution has a concentration of 0.5 mol/dm^3.
What is its concentration in g/dm^3?

Relative atomic masses (A_r): H = 1, O = 16, Na = 23

....

....

....

....

.... g/dm^3
[3]

10. Hydrogen-oxygen fuel cells involve a redox reaction.
Write the half equations that occur at the electrodes.

Anode: ....

Cathode: ....
[2]

11. Name the type of structure shown in the diagram.

....
[1]

12. When would a metal displace another metal from an aqueous solution of its salt?

....
[1]

Test 16: Rate and Extent of Chemical Change

There are **11 questions** in this test. Give yourself **10 minutes** to answer them all.

1. What is a reversible reaction?

   A A reaction where the products of the reaction can react to produce further products.

   B A reaction where the products of the reaction can react to produce the original reactants. [1]

2. When a reversible reaction occurs in a sealed reaction vessel, when is equilibrium reached?

   A When all the reactants are used up.

   B When the amounts of products and reactants are equal.

   C When the rates of the forward and reverse reactions are equal. [1]

3. How does a catalyst increase a reaction's rate?

   A It shifts the position of equilibrium.

   B It increases the energy of the reactants.

   C It decreases the activation energy needed. [1]

4. Which of these reactions would be faster?

   A Magnesium with concentrated acid

   B Magnesium with dilute acid [1]

5. The rate of a reaction doesn't depend on the...

   A ...frequency of collisions.

   B ...volume of solution.

   C ...temperature of the reactants. [1]

6. True or False? "A reversible reaction always takes in more energy in one direction than it gives out in the opposite direction."

   A True

   B False [1]

7. True or False? "Increasing the temperature of a reversible reaction will increase the yield of the exothermic reaction."

   A True

   B False [1]

8. Which of the following is not a unit of reaction rate?

   A g/s

   B cm^3/s

   C g/dm^3 [1]

9. The diagram shows the results of the same reaction carried out in two different experiments.

Suggest one way in which the conditions might have been different in experiment 2.
Explain your answer.

....

....

....
[2]

10. Magnesium reacts with hydrochloric acid to form magnesium chloride and hydrogen gas.
Describe how you could determine the mean rate of this reaction.

....

....

....

....
[3]

11. The equation below shows a reversible reaction, where A-D are different gases.

$$2A + B \rightleftharpoons C + D$$

Would the forwards or backwards reaction be favoured if the pressure were increased?
Explain your answer.

....

....

....
[2]

Topics for Paper 2: Rate and Extent of Chemical Change

Test 17: Rate and Extent of Chemical Change

There are **12 questions** in this test. Give yourself **10 minutes** to answer them all.

1. True or False? "The mean rate of reaction can be found by measuring the amount of reactant used over a period of time."

   A True
   B False
   [1]

2. Which of the following is a reason why increasing the temperature increases the rate of a reaction?

   A The reactant particles evaporate to form a gas.
   B The reactant particles move faster so they collide more frequently.
   C The reactant particles stick together more.
   [1]

3. True or False? "Different catalysts are needed for different reactions."

   A True
   B False
   [1]

4. In a reaction between marble and hydrochloric acid, using small marble chips instead of a large piece of marble will produce...

   A ...no difference in the rate of reaction.
   B ...a faster rate of reaction.
   C ...a slower rate of reaction.
   [1]

5. In a reversible reaction, increasing the concentration of reactants will favour the reaction that forms...

   A ...more product until equilibrium is reached again.
   B ...less product until equilibrium is reached again.
   [1]

6. What effect will decreasing the temperature have on the yield of the exothermic reaction in a reversible reaction?

   A Increase it
   B Decrease it
   C Have no effect
   [1]

7. Which of the following affects the proportion of collisions that have enough energy for particles to react?

   A Gas pressure
   B Temperature
   C Concentration
   [1]

8. Halving the frequency of collisions in a reaction mixture...

   A ...halves the reaction rate.
   B ...decreases reaction rate by a factor of 4.
   C ...doubles the reaction rate.
   [1]

Topics for Paper 2: Rate and Extent of Chemical Change

9. A reversible reaction is often said to be at equilibrium. What is meant by this?

   ....

   ....
   [1]

10. The equation for the decomposition of hydrogen peroxide is shown below:

    $$2H_2O_{2(aq)} \rightarrow 2H_2O_{(l)} + O_{2(g)}$$

    How would you expect the total volume of O_2 produced to be affected by the presence of a catalyst? Explain your answer.

    ....

    ....

    ....
    [2]

11. Explain, using collision theory, why increasing the concentration of a solution increases the rate of a reaction.

    ....

    ....

    ....
    [2]

12. In a reaction between calcium and water, 10.2 cm³ of hydrogen gas is collected over the first 20 seconds. Calculate the mean rate of reaction during this time.

    ....

    ....

    ....
    [2]

Test 18: Organic Chemistry

There are **12 questions** in this test. Give yourself **10 minutes** to answer them all.

1. Crude oil is a...

   A ...renewable resource.

   B ...finite resource.

   C ...infinite resource.
   [1]

2. What is the general formula of an alkane?

   A C_nH_{2n}

   B C_nH_{2n+2}

   C C_2H_6
   [1]

3. What happens to bromine water when an alkene is added to it?

   A It turns cloudy.

   B It turns from colourless to orange.

   C It turns from orange to colourless.
   [1]

4. Which of the methods below could be used to crack a long-chain hydrocarbon?

   A Mix the hydrocarbon with water and add a cold platinum catalyst.

   B Mix the hydrocarbon vapour with steam and heat to a very high temperature.
   [1]

5. What is produced when sugar solution is fermented using yeast?

   A Aqueous ethene and carbon dioxide

   B Nitrogen and aqueous ethanol

   C Carbon dioxide and aqueous ethanol
   [1]

6. What happens to the carbon and hydrogen in a fuel when it's burned?

   A They are oxidised.

   B They evaporate.

   C They react to form CH_4.
   [1]

7. Which of these is an ester?

   A Ethanoic acid

   B Ethyl ethanoate

   C Propanol
   [1]

8. True or False? "Carboxylic acids form very strong acids when dissolved in water."

   A True

   B False
   [1]

Topics for Paper 2: Organic Chemistry

9. Complete the word equation for the oxidation of ethanol:

ethanol + oxygen → .... + water

[1]

10. Why are alkenes described as unsaturated?

....

....

[1]

11. Name the type of reaction shown below and explain why ethene can undergo this reaction.

$$n \begin{pmatrix} H & H \\ | & | \\ C = C \\ | & | \\ H & H \end{pmatrix} \longrightarrow \begin{pmatrix} H & H \\ | & | \\ -C - C- \\ | & | \\ H & H \end{pmatrix}_n$$

ethene → poly(ethene)

....

....

[2]

12. The compound shown reacts with sodium carbonate to form a salt.
Name the compound shown and state the other products formed in its reaction with sodium carbonate.

Name: ....

Other products formed: ....

[3]

Test 19: Organic Chemistry

There are **11 questions** in this test. Give yourself **10 minutes** to answer them all.

1. Which technique is used to separate the components of crude oil?

   A Cracking

   B Filtration

   C Fractional distillation

   [1]

2. What product is formed when ethene reacts with iodine?

   A CH_2ICH_2I

   B CH_5I

   C CH_2CHI

   [1]

3. True or False? "Condensation polymerisation involves monomers with a single functional group."

   A True

   B False

   [1]

4. Which of the following statements about amino acids is true?

   A They contain one functional group.

   B They undergo addition polymerisation.

   C They undergo condensation polymerisation.

   [1]

5. True or False? "DNA is made up of one polymer chain called a nucleotide."

   A True

   B False

   [1]

6. Which of these is not an alcohol?

   A Methanol

   B Butane

   C Propanol

   [1]

7. True or False? "Cracking is used to turn long-chain hydrocarbons into short-chain hydrocarbons."

   A True

   B False

   [1]

8. What is produced when ethene is hydrated with steam in the presence of a catalyst?

   A Ethanol

   B Water

   C Oxygen

   [1]

Topics for Paper 2: Organic Chemistry

9. Write a balanced symbol equation for the complete combustion of propane, C_3H_8.

....
[2]

10. The formulas of two alkanes, decane and pentane, are shown below:

Decane: $C_{10}H_{22}$

Pentane: C_5H_{12}

Which of these alkanes will have the higher boiling point?
Explain your answer.

....

....
[2]

11. Vaporised crude oil is piped into the bottom of a fractionating column.
Explain how it is then separated into different fractions.

....

....

....

....

....
[3]

Test 20: Chemical Analysis

There are **12 questions** in this test. Give yourself **10 minutes** to answer them all.

1. What colour is the flame produced when a calcium compound is burnt in a flame test?

   A Green

   B Orange-Red

   C Yellow
   [1]

2. What colour is silver iodide?

   A Cream

   B White

   C Yellow
   [1]

3. True or False? "Limewater is used to test for hydrogen gas."

   A True

   B False
   [1]

4. Which of these metal ions does not form a white precipitate in a reaction with sodium hydroxide solution?

   A Magnesium ions

   B Calcium ions

   C Iron(II) ions
   [1]

5. What solutions are normally used to test for sulfate ions?

   A Dilute hydrochloric acid and barium chloride solution.

   B Dilute nitric acid and barium chloride solution.
   [1]

6. What gas will be released when dilute hydrochloric acid is added to a solution of sodium carbonate?

   A Hydrogen

   B Carbon dioxide

   C Methane
   [1]

7. How many different phases are used in chromatography?

   A 1

   B 2

   C 3
   [1]

8. True or False? "Oxygen will relight a glowing splint."

   A True

   B False
   [1]

Topics for Paper 2: Chemical Analysis

9. Dilute nitric acid is added to a solution containing chloride ions (Cl⁻), followed by a few drops of silver nitrate solution.
Name the solid substance that is formed during this reaction and state its colour.

....

....
[2]

10. Give two advantages of using instrumental analysis, such as flame emission spectroscopy, instead of chemical tests to identify unknown substances.

....

....
[2]

11. A student carried out a series of tests on an unknown compound.

Here are the results of the tests:

Adding sodium hydroxide to a solution of the compound produced a green precipitate.

Adding dilute nitric acid and then silver nitrate to a solution of the compound produced a cream precipitate.

Identify the:

metal ion present in the compound ....

non-metal ion present in the compound ....
[2]

12. Describe the chemical test for chlorine.

....
[1]

Test 21: Chemical Analysis

There are **12 questions** in this test. Give yourself **10 minutes** to answer them all.

1. What is the test for hydrogen?

   A It burns with a green flame.

   B It turns damp litmus paper white.

   C It burns with a pop.
   [1]

2. When carbon dioxide is bubbled through limewater, the limewater turns...

   A ...cloudy.

   B ...green.

   C ...yellow.
   [1]

3. True or False? "Copper(II) ions form a white precipitate in a reaction with sodium hydroxide solution."

   A True

   B False
   [1]

4. True or False? "Formulations are made for a specific purpose by mixing together exact amounts of different components."

   A True

   B False
   [1]

5. Which of the following statements about flame emission spectroscopy is true?

   A It cannot be used to identify the concentration of ions in solution.

   B It can identify several metal ions in a compound.

   C It is less reliable than flame tests.
   [1]

6. A cream precipitate is formed when dilute nitric acid then silver nitrate solution are added to a solution. What does this show?

   A The solution contains chloride ions.

   B The solution contains iodide ions.

   C The solution contains bromide ions.
   [1]

7. In chromatography...

   A ...the mobile phase moves through the stationary phase.

   B ...the substances in the sample do not move between the phases.
   [1]

8. In a flame test, which metal compounds burn to give a yellow flame?

   A Calcium

   B Potassium

   C Sodium
   [1]

Topics for Paper 2: Chemical Analysis

9. How could you use sodium hydroxide to distinguish between solutions of aluminium chloride and calcium chloride?

....

....

....
[2]

10. Complete the following method to test for the presence of sulfate ions in a compound.

   1. Add dilute hydrochloric acid to a solution of the compound.

   2. ....

   3. A .... precipitate will form if the compound contains sulfate ions.
   [2]

11. A student carries out paper chromatography on a pure substance. The solvent travelled 5 cm up the chromatography paper. The substance left a spot 3.2 cm up the chromatography paper. What is the R_f value of the substance?

....

....

....
[2]

12. The melting point of a sample of water is found −2 °C. Suggest why this is.

....
[1]

Test 22: Chemistry of the Atmosphere

There are **11 questions** in this test. Give yourself **10 minutes** to answer them all.

1. Why is sulfur often removed from fuels before they are burnt?

   A So the fuel produces less soot when it burns.

   B To reduce the cost of the fuel.

   C To reduce acid rain.
   [1]

2. Which of these is not produced when a fuel undergoes complete combustion?

   A Carbon monoxide

   B Carbon dioxide

   C Water
   [1]

3. Which of these is thought to be increasing the average global temperature?

   A An increasing amount of greenhouse gases in the atmosphere.

   B An increased amount of particulates in the atmosphere from car emissions.

   C Large amounts of sulfur dioxide gas being released from burning fuels.
   [1]

4. It is difficult for scientists to be certain what the implications of global climate change will be because...

   A ...the evidence has not been peer-reviewed.

   B ...the Earth's climate is very complicated so is hard to model.

   C ...media reports are biased.
   [1]

5. True or False? "Nitrogen oxides form when fuels burn slowly at low temperatures."

   A True

   B False
   [1]

6. Which of the following is formed mainly from shells and skeletons of marine organisms?

   A Limestone

   B Coal

   C Crude oil
   [1]

7. Which of these gases is not a greenhouse gas?

   A Water vapour

   B Methane

   C Oxygen
   [1]

8. What percentage of the Earth's atmosphere is made up of oxygen?

   A About 80%

   B About 20%

   C Less than 1%
   [1]

Topics for Paper 2: Chemistry of the Atmosphere

9. Describe one way that governments can reduce carbon dioxide emissions.
Give one reason why their actions are limited.

....

....

....

.... *[2]*

10. Explain how the evolution of algae and green plants affected the composition of Earth's atmosphere.

....

....

.... *[2]*

11. Which gas made up most of the Earth's early atmosphere?

....

Name one other gas present in the Earth's early atmosphere.

....

Where did these gases come from?

.... *[3]*

Test 23: Chemistry of the Atmosphere

There are **10 questions** in this test. Give yourself **10 minutes** to answer them all.

1. True or False? "Greenhouse gases in the atmosphere help to keep temperatures on Earth high enough to support life."

   A   True

   B   False

   [1]

2. Which of these gases makes up the smallest proportion of our atmosphere?

   A   Oxygen

   B   Nitrogen

   C   Carbon dioxide

   [1]

3. True or False? "The carbon footprint of the power we use can be reduced by using nuclear energy rather than fossil fuels."

   A   True

   B   False

   [1]

4. Solid particles in the atmosphere block some sunlight from reaching the Earth's surface. What is this effect called?

   A   Global warming

   B   Global dimming

   C   Shadowing

   [1]

5. Carbon monoxide is...

   A   ...a toxic gas.

   B   ...a hydrocarbon.

   C   ...a cause of acid rain.

   [1]

6. Which of these gases can cause respiratory problems?

   A   Sulfur dioxide

   B   Nitrogen

   C   Carbon Dioxide

   [1]

7. Which of the following is not a reason that carbon dioxide levels decreased in the Earth's early atmosphere?

   A   The formation of sedimentary rocks and fossil fuels that contain carbon.

   B   The carbon dioxide reacted with oxygen in the atmosphere.

   C   Algae and plants began to photosynthesise.

   [1]

8. Greenhouse gases...

   A   ...absorb all wavelengths of radiation.

   B   ...absorb short wavelength radiation from the Sun.

   C   ...absorb long wavelength radiation from the Earth.

   [1]

Topics for Paper 2: Chemistry of the Atmosphere

9. How may rising global temperatures affect the polar ice caps?
Describe the consequences that this may have.

....

....

....

....
[3]

10. Give two human activities that increase the amount of methane in the atmosphere.
For each, explain why it causes an increase.

1. ....

....

2. ....

....
[4]

Topics for Paper 2: Chemistry of the Atmosphere

Test 24: Using Resources

There are **11 questions** in this test. Give yourself **10 minutes** to answer them all.

1. The main goal of a life cycle assessment is to assess...

   A ...the total environmental cost of a product.

   B ...the economic impact of a product.

   C ...how long a product will be in use.
   [1]

2. Why is bioleaching used to extract copper from its ore?

   A It's quicker than electrolysis.

   B It produces copper with fewer impurities than electrolysis.

   C It can be used on low-grade ores.
   [1]

3. Which of these isn't a raw material used in the Haber process?

   A Hydrogen

   B Nitrogen

   C Oxygen
   [1]

4. Which of these will not affect the properties of a polymer?

   A The monomers from which it is made.

   B The reaction conditions that it is made under.

   C The quantity made during production.
   [1]

5. NPK fertilisers are formulations containing salts of...

   A ...nitrogen, phosphorus and potassium.

   B ...nitrogen, potassium and krypton.

   C ...copper, nitrogen and potassium.
   [1]

6. What is electroplating?

   A Removing the surface of a metal object.

   B Coating an object with a thin layer of metal.

   C Creating an electric plate.
   [1]

7. True or False? "Unlike metals, glass cannot be recycled."

   A True

   B False
   [1]

8. True or False? "Aluminium alloys have a high density but are resistant to corrosion."

   A True

   B False
   [1]

Topics for Paper 2: Using Resources

9. Describe two environmental impacts of extracting a metal from its ore.

   1. ....

   ....

   2. ....

   ....
   [2]

10. Potable water can be produced from fresh water. This process involves sterilising the water to kill any harmful bacteria or microbes.
    Give two ways in which water can be sterilised.

    1. ....

    2. ....
    [2]

11. The Haber process uses an exothermic reaction to produce ammonia.
    Explain why the reaction is carried out at a moderately high temperature (450 °C).

    ....

    ....

    ....

    ....
    [3]

Topics for Paper 2: Using Resources

Test 25: Using Resources

There are **11 questions** in this test. Give yourself **10 minutes** to answer them all.

1. What is phytomining?

   A A process that uses displacement reactions to extract copper.

   B A process that uses bacteria to separate metals from low-grade ores.

   C A process that uses plants to separate metals from low-grade ores.
   [1]

2. Which process produces sewage sludge and effluent during sewage treatment?

   A Screening

   B Biological aerobic digestion

   C Sedimentation
   [1]

3. True or False? "Steel is an alloy made of iron, oxygen and sulfur."

   A True

   B False
   [1]

4. True or False? "The nitrogen used in the Haber process is obtained from air."

   A True

   B False
   [1]

5. True or False? "A life cycle assessment is an objective way to assess the environmental impact of a product and remove bias."

   A True

   B False
   [1]

6. Thermosetting polymers have...

   A ...polymer chains with cross-links.

   B ...tangled polymer chains.

   C ...weak intermolecular forces.
   [1]

7. True or False? "To be described as potable, water must contain no dissolved salts."

   A True

   B False
   [1]

8. Which of the following is an example of a renewable resource?

   A Copper

   B Wool

   C Nuclear fuel such as uranium
   [1]

Topics for Paper 2: Using Resources

9. Phosphate rock is reacted with sulfuric acid to produce salts that are used in fertilisers. Name the two salts that are produced in this reaction.

   1. ....

   2. ....
   [2]

10. Describe the key feature of most composites.

    ....

    ....
    [1]

11. What are the four stages of a product's life that are examined during a life cycle assessment?

    1. ....

    2. ....

    3. ....

    4. ....
    [4]

15

Topics for Paper 2: Using Resources

Test 26: Paper 2 Mixed Topics

There are **11 questions** in this test. Give yourself **10 minutes** to answer them all.

1. True or False? "Increasing the pressure of the reaction $N_{2(g)} + 3H_{2(g)} \rightleftharpoons 2NH_{3(g)}$ favours the forward reaction."

   A True
   B False
   [1]

2. How many hydrogen atoms does ethane contain?

   A 2
   B 6
   C 8
   [1]

3. True or False? "Oxygen is the most abundant gas in the atmosphere."

   A True
   B False
   [1]

4. True or False? "Thermosetting polymers melt when heated."

   A True
   B False
   [1]

5. On a graph showing the quantity of product formed against time, a tangent to the curve gives the...

   A ...concentration of the product.
   B ...mean rate of reaction.
   C ...rate of reaction at a specific time.
   [1]

6. Which of the following is true for condensation polymerisation?

   A For each new bond that forms a small molecule is usually lost.
   B The product is collected through condensation.
   C The monomers contain a C=C bond.
   [1]

7. Which of these processes can be used to desalinate sea water?

   A Sterilisation
   B Reverse osmosis
   C Sedimentation
   [1]

8. What gas is produced when butanol reacts with sodium?

   A Carbon dioxide
   B Oxygen
   C Hydrogen
   [1]

9. Name the compound on the right and state two uses of it.

$$\begin{array}{c} H \\ | \\ H-C-O-H \\ | \\ H \end{array}$$

Name: ....

Uses: 1. ....

2. ....
[3]

10. Explain how the pattern of spots produced in a chromatography experiment can be used to distinguish a pure substance from an impure substance.

....

....
[2]

11. What is Le Chatelier's principle?

....

....
[2]

Test 27: Paper 2 Mixed Topics

There are **11 questions** in this test. Give yourself **10 minutes** to answer them all.

1. True or False? "Iron(III) ions form a brown precipitate in a reaction with sodium hydroxide solution."

   A True

   B False

   [1]

2. What are the two functional groups on an amino acid?

   A An NH_2 group and a COOH group

   B Two NH_2 groups

   C An NH_2 group and an OH group

   [1]

3. True or False? "Chemical reactions all happen at the same speed."

   A True

   B False

   [1]

4. Why is zinc sometimes used to coat iron?

   A It is less reactive than iron so provides a protective coating around the iron.

   B It is more reactive than iron so water and oxygen will react with it instead of with the iron.

   C It is decorative.

   [1]

5. What is DNA?

   A A molecule with an amino group and a carboxyl group.

   B A polymer made up of amino acids.

   C Two polymer chains connected by cross links.

   [1]

6. What change in the early atmosphere of earth made it possible for animals to evolve?

   A A decrease of nitrogen.

   B An increase of carbon dioxide.

   C An increase of oxygen.

   [1]

7. True or False? "Changes in the Earth's climate may affect the ability of certain regions to produce food."

   A True

   B False

   [1]

8. Ethyl ethanoate is produced by reacting ethanol with...

   A ...ethane.

   B ...ethanoic acid.

   C ...ethene.

   [1]

9. State one difference between the properties of soda-lime glass and the properties of borosilicate glass.

   ....

   .... [1]

10. A certain reaction is carried out with and without a catalyst.
    Which line on the graph shows the reaction with a catalyst? Explain your answer.

    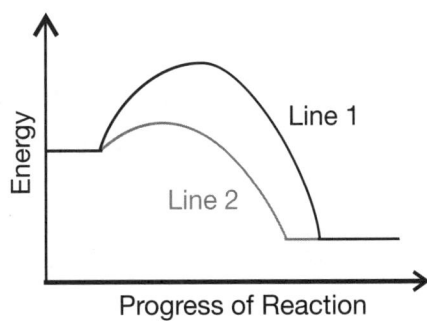

    ....

    .... [2]

11. Describe how greenhouse gases cause the warming of the surface of the Earth.

    ....

    ....

    ....

    .... [4]

Test 28: Paper 2 Mixed Topics

There are **11 questions** in this test. Give yourself **10 minutes** to answer them all.

1. True or False? "Catalysts are used up during a reaction."

   A True
   B False
   [1]

2. True or False? "Short-chain hydrocarbons are more useful than long-chain hydrocarbons."

   A True
   B False
   [1]

3. In a flame test, which metal compounds burn to give a green flame?

   A Copper
   B Calcium
   C Potassium
   [1]

4. What is borosilicate glass made from?

   A Sand and boron trioxide
   B Sand, sodium carbonate and limestone.
   C Sand, boron and sodium carbonate.
   [1]

5. A small amount of dilute acid is added to an unknown solution. A gas is produced which turns limewater milky. Which of the following might the unknown solution contain?

   A Butene
   B Sodium carbonate
   C Sodium chloride
   [1]

6. What is the first stage in making fresh water safe to drink?

   A Filtration
   B Distillation
   C Sterilisation
   [1]

7. Which of the following increases the rate of reaction?

   A Diluting the solution in which the reaction is happening.
   B Measuring the amount of gas evolved each second.
   C Increasing the average energy of the collisions.
   [1]

8. Which of these effects on the planet is not associated with burning fossil fuels?

   A An increase in the average global temperature.
   B An increase in the amount of oxygen in the oceans.
   C An increase in the amount of carbon dioxide in the atmosphere.
   [1]

9. Describe an experiment to show that both air and water are needed for rusting to occur.

....

....

....

....
[4]

10. What is a selective life cycle assessment and how might it be misused by a company?

....

....

....
[2]

11. Ethanol can be produced by fermentation using yeast.
State the optimum temperature for this process.

....
[1]

Test 29: Paper 2 Mixed Topics

There are **11 questions** in this test. Give yourself **10 minutes** to answer them all.

1. Which of the following are produced by cracking?

   A   Alkanes and water vapour

   B   Alkanes and alkenes

   C   Only alkanes

   [1]

2. True or False? "Taxing companies based on the amount of greenhouse gases they produce aims to increase the country's carbon footprint."

   A   True

   B   False

   [1]

3. When ethanol is oxidised, it produces...

   A   ...an ester.

   B   ...ethanoic acid.

   C   ...sodium polymer.

   [1]

4. True or False? "The Haber process is carried out at a very low temperature."

   A   True

   B   False

   [1]

5. Which of these metal ions forms a white precipitate in a reaction with sodium hydroxide solution?

   A   Calcium ions

   B   Copper(II) ions

   C   Iron(II) ions

   [1]

6. Decreasing the pressure of a gaseous reversible reaction at equilibrium will cause the equilibrium to...

   A   ...move in the direction where there are fewer molecules of gas.

   B   ...move in the endothermic direction.

   C   ...move in the direction where there are more molecules of gas.

   [1]

7. Which of these is used to test for the presence of an alkene?

   A   Limewater

   B   Bromine water

   C   Sodium hydroxide solution

   [1]

8. After bioleaching, further processing is required to obtain copper metal. Which of these processes is not used for this?

   A   Electrolysis

   B   Phytomining

   C   Displacement by iron

   [1]

Mixed Tests for Paper 2

9. Name the alloy produced when tin is added to pure copper. Give one use of it.

   Alloy: ....

   Use: ....
   [2]

10. Complete and balance the chemical equation for the combustion of methanol.

    ....CH_3OH + ...O_2 → ....CO_2 + ...
    [2]

11. Using collision theory, explain how breaking a solid reactant up into smaller pieces will affect the rate of a reaction.

    ....

    ....

    ....

    ....
    [3]

15

Test 30: Paper 2 Mixed Topics

There are **10 questions** in this test. Give yourself **10 minutes** to answer them all.

1. True or False? "Increasing the pressure of any reaction mixture will increase the reaction rate."

   A True
   B False
   [1]

2. You can test for halide ions by adding dilute nitric acid to a solution followed by...

   A ...limewater.
   B ...silver nitrate solution.
   C ...sodium hydroxide solution.
   [1]

3. How is ammonia removed during the Haber process?

   A By adding gases that react with the hydrogen and nitrogen.
   B By fractional distillation.
   C By cooling to liquefy it.
   [1]

4. If a reversible reaction is endothermic in one direction what will it be in the other?

   A Endothermic
   B Could be exothermic or endothermic
   C Exothermic
   [1]

5. True or False? "In chromatography, the R_f value for a substance will be the same no matter what solvent is used."

   A True
   B False
   [1]

6. What type of hydrocarbon burns with a smoky flame?

   A Alkanes
   B Alkenes
   C Alcohols
   [1]

7. Which of the following cannot be used in showing that a sample of a substance is impure?

   A Melting or boiling point data
   B Chromatography
   C Crystallisation
   [1]

8. Why can the hydrocarbons in crude oil be separated by fractional distillation?

   A They have different boiling points.
   B They have different melting points.
   C They have different viscosities.
   [1]

9. Why is a high pressure of 200 atmospheres used for the Haber process?
Explain its effect on both reaction rate and yield.

....

....

....
[3]

10. Sedimentation is one of the processes used in sewage treatment.
During sedimentation, the sewage separates into two parts.
Name each part and state the process used to treated it.

Part 1: ....

Process used to treat it: ....

Part 2: ....

Process used to treat it: ....
[4]

Answers

Topics for Paper 1

Test 1: Atomic Structure and the Periodic Table
Pages 2–3
1. B *[1 mark]*   2. A *[1 mark]*
3. A *[1 mark]*   4. B *[1 mark]*
5. C *[1 mark]*   6. A *[1 mark]*
7. B *[1 mark]*   8. A *[1 mark]*
9. They have the same number of outer electrons/electrons in their outer shell *[1 mark]*.
10. Isotopes are different forms of the same element, which have the same number of protons but a different number of neutrons *[1 mark]*.
11. Electron — negative / −1 *[1 mark]*
    Proton — positive / +1 *[1 mark]*
    Neutron — no charge / 0 *[1 mark]*
12. As you move down the group, the outer electron is further away from the nucleus *[1 mark]*. So it is less strongly attracted to the nucleus and is lost more easily *[1 mark]*.

Test 2: Atomic Structure and the Periodic Table
Pages 4–5
1. C *[1 mark]*   2. B *[1 mark]*
3. A *[1 mark]*   4. C *[1 mark]*
5. C *[1 mark]*   6. B *[1 mark]*
7. C *[1 mark]*   8. C *[1 mark]*
9. It's got too many electrons in the first shell/The first shell should only hold two electrons *[1 mark]*. The third shell has started filling before the second shell is full/The second shell should hold eight electrons before the third shell starts to fill *[1 mark]*.
10. Any three of: e.g. Transition metals have higher melting points. / Transition metals are denser. / Transition metals are stronger. / Transition metals are harder. / Transition metals are less reactive. / Transition metals form multiple ions. / Transition metals form coloured compounds *[1 mark each]*.
11. A reaction would occur if the pure halogen was more reactive than the halogen in the salt. *[1 mark]*

12. $2Li + 2H_2O \rightarrow 2LiOH + H_2$ *[1 mark]*.

Test 3: Bonding, Structure and Properties
Pages 6–7
1. C *[1 mark]*   2. A *[1 mark]*
3. B *[1 mark]*   4. A *[1 mark]*
5. C *[1 mark]*   6. B *[1 mark]*
7. B *[1 mark]*   8. A *[1 mark]*
9. The two chlorine atoms share a pair of electrons *[1 mark]*. This forms a single covalent bond *[1 mark]*.
10. Sodium chloride is a giant ionic lattice *[1 mark]*, made up of sodium ions and chloride ions *[1 mark]*.
11. The intermolecular forces between polymer molecules are large, so a lot of energy is needed to break them apart *[1 mark]*.
12. Graphite has free/delocalised electrons between layers *[1 mark]* that can move and carry a charge *[1 mark]*.

Test 4: Bonding, Structure and Properties
Pages 8–9
1. A *[1 mark]*   2. B *[1 mark]*
3. C *[1 mark]*   4. B *[1 mark]*
5. C *[1 mark]*   6. B *[1 mark]*
7. B *[1 mark]*   8. A *[1 mark]*
9. The metal atom loses electrons to form a positively charged ion and the non-metal gains these electrons to form negatively charged ion. *[1 mark]*.
10. Fullerenes are molecules of carbon atoms that form hollow shapes *[1 mark]*. The carbon atoms are arranged in hexagonal rings (but can also contain rings with 5 or 7 carbon atoms) *[1 mark]*. They are used e.g. for drug delivery into the body / in lubricants / as catalysts / as nanotubes *[1 mark]*.
11. Any two of: e.g. drugs / electronic circuits / cosmetics / suncreams / deodorants / catalysts *[1 mark each]*.
12. Ethanol (it boils at 78°C) *[1 mark]*.

Test 5: Quantitative Chemistry
Pages 10–11
1. B *[1 mark]*   2. B *[1 mark]*
3. A *[1 mark]*   4. B *[1 mark]*
5. B *[1 mark]*   6. A *[1 mark]*
7. B *[1 mark]*   8. C *[1 mark]*
9. Relative formula mass (M_r)
   $= 24 + (2 \times 16) + (2 \times 1) = 58$ *[1 mark]*
   Mass = number of moles $\times M_r$
   $= 2.5 \times 58$ *[1 mark]*
   $= 145$ g *[1 mark]*
   [Or 3 marks for the correct answer via any other method.]
10. Convert 25.0 cm³ and 40.0 cm³ to dm³:
    Volume of KOH = 25.0 ÷ 1000
    = 0.0250 dm³
    Volume of H_2SO_4 = 40.0 ÷ 1000
    = 0.0400 dm³
    [1 mark]
    Number of moles of KOH
    = concentration × volume
    = 0.200 × 0.0250 *[1 mark]*
    = 0.00500 mol
    From the equation, 2 moles of KOH reacts with 1 mole of H_2SO_4, so there were 0.00500 ÷ 2 = 0.00250 moles of H_2SO_4 in the acid solution *[1 mark]*.
    So acid concentration = moles ÷ volume = 0.00250 ÷ 0.0400
    = 0.0625 mol/dm³ *[1 mark]*
    [Or 4 marks for the correct answer via any other method.]

Test 6: Quantitative Chemistry
Pages 12–13
1. A *[1 mark]*   2. A *[1 mark]*
3. B *[1 mark]*   4. C *[1 mark]*
5. C *[1 mark]*   6. B *[1 mark]*
7. A *[1 mark]*   8. A *[1 mark]*
9. Percentage yield = (actual yield ÷ theoretical yield) × 100
   = (36 ÷ 50) × 100 *[1 mark]*
   = 72% *[1 mark]*
   [Or 2 marks for the correct answer via any other method.]

Answers

10. 0.00025 kg × 1000 = 0.25 g
    Concentration = mass ÷ volume
    = 0.25 ÷ 0.5 *[1 mark]*
    = 0.5 g/dm³ *[1 mark]*
    [Or 2 marks for the correct answer via any other method.]
11. Divide the reacting mass of iron by its A_r and divide the reacting mass of oxygen gas by its M_r to give the number of moles:
    Fe: 280 ÷ 56 = 5.0 moles
    O₂: 80 ÷ 32 = 2.5 moles *[1 mark]*
    So 5.0 moles of Fe reacts with 2.5 moles of O₂. This simplifies to 2:1 *[1 mark]*. So the symbol equation is 2Fe + O₂ → 2FeO *[1 mark]*.
    [Or 3 marks for the correct answer via any other method.]

Test 7: Chemical Changes
Pages 14–15

1. C *[1 mark]*   2. A *[1 mark]*
3. A *[1 mark]*   4. B *[1 mark]*
5. C *[1 mark]*   6. C *[1 mark]*
7. A *[1 mark]*   8. B *[1 mark]*
9. hydrogen *[1 mark]* and chlorine *[1 mark]*
10. $H^+_{(aq)} + OH^-_{(aq)} \rightarrow H_2O_{(l)}$ *[1 mark]*
11. Negative electrode: aluminium ions are reduced/gain electrons to form aluminium / $Al^{3+} + 3e^- \rightarrow Al$ *[1 mark]*
    Positive electrode: oxygen ions are oxidised/lose electrons to form oxygen / $2O^{2-} \rightarrow O_2 + 4e^-$ *[1 mark]*
12. The positive electrode is made of carbon *[1 mark]*. This 'wears away' as it reacts with the oxygen produced during electrolysis, forming carbon dioxide *[1 mark]*.

Test 8: Chemical Changes
Pages 16–17

1. B *[1 mark]*   2. A *[1 mark]*
3. A *[1 mark]*   4. B *[1 mark]*
5. C *[1 mark]*   6. B *[1 mark]*
7. B *[1 mark]*   8. C *[1 mark]*
9. copper chloride *[1 mark]* and water *[1 mark]*.

10. Metal: Any metal that's above carbon in the reactivity series, e.g. aluminium *[1 mark]*.
    Explanation: It's extracted by electrolysis because it's too reactive to be extracted by reduction with carbon/ it is above carbon in the reactivity series *[1 mark]*.
11. Magnesium reacts vigorously with hydrochloric acid, producing bubbles/effervescence *[1 mark]*. The reaction of HCl with iron would be less vigorous/produce fewer bubbles than with magnesium *[1 mark]*. This is because magnesium is more reactive than iron / is higher than iron in the reactivity series *[1 mark]*.

Test 9: Energy Changes
Pages 18–19

1. C *[1 mark]*   2. B *[1 mark]*
3. A *[1 mark]*   4. A *[1 mark]*
5. B *[1 mark]*   6. B *[1 mark]*
7. B *[1 mark]*   8. C *[1 mark]*
9. Find the energy required to break the bonds:
   4(C – H) + 2(O = O)
   = (4 × 413) + (2 × 496)
   = 2644 kJ/mol *[1 mark]*
   Find the energy released when forming new bonds:
   2(C = O) + 4(O – H)
   = (2 × 803) + (4 × 464)
   = 3462 kJ/mol *[1 mark]*
   So the energy change =
   2644 – 3462 = –818 kJ/mol *[1 mark]*
   [Or 3 marks for the correct answer via any other method.]
10. Any two of: e.g. batteries are more polluting to dispose of as they're made from toxic metal compounds / fuel cells are less expensive to make / fuel cells store more energy so don't need to be recharged often *[1 mark for each]*.
11. It shows an exothermic reaction *[1 mark]*. You can tell this because the products are at a lower energy than the reactants *[1 mark]*.

Test 10: Energy Changes
Pages 20–21

1. A *[1 mark]*   2. A *[1 mark]*
3. A *[1 mark]*   4. A *[1 mark]*
5. B *[1 mark]*   6. A *[1 mark]*
7. C *[1 mark]*   8. A *[1 mark]*
9.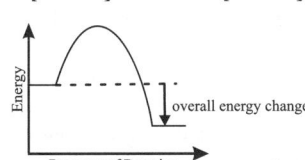
   [1 mark for correct axes, 1 mark for correct labelling overall energy change, 1 mark for correct shape of curve linking the reactants to the products.]
10. Any two of: e.g. combustion / oxidation / neutralisation *[1 mark for each]*.
11. The metal in cell 1 is the most reactive *[1 mark]*. The smallest voltage was produced in that cell, so this metal had the smallest difference in reactivity between itself and sodium *[1 mark]*.

Mixed Tests for Paper 1

Test 11: Paper 1 Mixed Topics
Pages 22–23

1. B *[1 mark]*   2. A *[1 mark]*
3. B *[1 mark]*   4. A *[1 mark]*
5. C *[1 mark]*   6. A *[1 mark]*
7. A *[1 mark]*   8. B *[1 mark]*
9. Relative formula mass (M_r)
   = (2 × 23) + 12 + (3 × 16) = 106 *[1 mark]*
   Moles = mass ÷ M_r = 50 ÷ 106 *[1 mark]*
   = 0.472 mol *[1 mark]*
   [Or 3 marks for the correct answer via any other method.]
10. A (metal) salt *[1 mark]* and hydrogen *[1 mark]*.
11. Group 4 *[1 mark]*, as it has four electrons in its outer shell *[1 mark]*.

Answers

Test 12: Paper 1 Mixed Topics
Pages 24–25
1. C *[1 mark]* 2. A *[1 mark]*
3. B *[1 mark]* 4. A *[1 mark]*
5. A *[1 mark]* 6. B *[1 mark]*
7. C *[1 mark]* 8. B *[1 mark]*
9. The reactions in rechargeable batteries are reversed when an external current is supplied *[1 mark]*. In non-rechargeable batteries, the reactions aren't reversible and the reactants are eventually used up *[1 mark]*.
10. 2 moles of oxygen → 1 mole of carbon dioxide, therefore 2 volumes of oxygen → 1 volume of carbon dioxide *[1 mark]*. So the volume of carbon dioxide formed = 120 ÷ 2 = 60 dm^3 *[1 mark]*.
1 mole of gas = 24 dm^3, so 60 dm^3 = 60 ÷ 24 = 2.5 moles of gas *[1 mark]*.
Mass of CO_2 = moles × M_r = 2.5 × 44 = 110 g *[1 mark]*.
[Or 4 marks for the correct answer via any other method.]
11. Strong acids ionise completely in water, weak acids do not fully ionise in water *[1 mark]*.

Test 13: Paper 1 Mixed Topics
Pages 26–27
1. B *[1 mark]* 2. A *[1 mark]*
3. B *[1 mark]* 4. C *[1 mark]*
5. A *[1 mark]* 6. C *[1 mark]*
7. A *[1 mark]* 8. A *[1 mark]*
9. An ionic compound has a giant ionic lattice structure *[1 mark]* that's held together by electrostatic forces of attraction between the oppositely charged ions *[1 mark]*.
10. Atom economy = (relative formula mass of desired products ÷ relative formula mass of all reactants) × 100
= [(24 + (35.5 × 2)) ÷ (24 + (2 × (1 + 35.5))] × 100
= [95 ÷ 97] × 100 *[1 mark]*.
Atom economy = 97.9% (to 1 d.p.) *[1 mark]*.

11. Relative formula mass (M_r) of CO_2 = 12 + (2 × 16) = 44 *[1 mark]*.
Number of moles of C = 66 g ÷ 12 = 5.5. From balanced equation, 5.5 moles of CO_2 are produced *[1 mark]*.
Mass of CO_2 = moles × M_r = 5.5 × 44 = 242 g *[1 mark]*.
[Or 3 marks for the correct answer via any other method.]

Test 14: Paper 1 Mixed Topics
Pages 28–29
1. B *[1 mark]* 2. A *[1 mark]*
3. B *[1 mark]* 4. A *[1 mark]*
5. B *[1 mark]* 6. C *[1 mark]*
7. A *[1 mark]* 8. B *[1 mark]*
9. Put the alkali in a flask with an indicator *[1 mark]*. Put the acid in a burette *[1 mark]*. Add the contents of the burette to the flask a bit at a time, swirling the flask regularly *[1 mark]*. Stop when the indicator changes colour, and record the volume of acid from the burette that was needed to neutralise the contents of the flask *[1 mark]*.
10. Find the number of moles in 1.84 g of ethanol:
moles = mass ÷ M_r
= 1.84 ÷ 46 = 0.04 moles *[1 mark]*
1 mole of ethanol reacts to form 2 moles of carbon dioxide, so 0.04 moles reacts to form 0.04 × 2 = 0.08 moles *[1 mark]*
[Or 2 marks for the correct answer via any other method.]
11. Many transition metal compounds are coloured *[1 mark]*.

Test 15: Paper 1 Mixed Topics
Pages 30–31
1. A *[1 mark]* 2. C *[1 mark]*
3. B *[1 mark]* 4. B *[1 mark]*
5. A *[1 mark]* 6. B *[1 mark]*
7. A *[1 mark]* 8. B *[1 mark]*

9. M_r of NaOH = 23 + 16 + 1 = 40 *[1 mark]*
mass = moles × M_r = 0.5 × 40 = 20 g *[1 mark]*
This is the mass per dm^3, so the concentration is 20 g/dm^3 *[1 mark]*.
[Or 3 marks for the correct answer via any other method.]
10. Anode: $H_2 \rightarrow 2H^+ + 2e^-$ *[1 mark]*
Cathode: $O_2 + 4H^+ + 4e^- \rightarrow 2H_2O$ *[1 mark]*
11. giant covalent *[1 mark]*
12. A metal will displace another metal if it's more reactive *[1 mark]*.

Topics for Paper 2

Test 16: Rate and Extent of Chemical Change
Pages 32–33
1. B *[1 mark]* 2. C *[1 mark]*
3. C *[1 mark]* 4. A *[1 mark]*
5. B *[1 mark]* 6. B *[1 mark]*
7. B *[1 mark]* 8. C *[1 mark]*
9. E.g. Experiment 2 could have been carried out at a higher temperature / with a greater concentration of reactants / at a higher pressure (with gases) / with a catalyst / with solid reactants crushed into smaller parts *[1 mark]*. This would have increased the rate of reaction, as shown by the steeper graph *[1 mark]*.
10. E.g. carry out the reaction on a mass balance and record the decrease in mass *[1 mark]* and the time it takes for the reaction to finish *[1 mark]*. Calculate the mean rate of reaction by dividing the decrease in mass by the time taken *[1 mark]*. / Using a gas syringe, record the volume of gas given off *[1 mark]* and the time it takes for the reaction to finish *[1 mark]*. Calculate the mean rate of reaction by dividing the volume of gas by the time taken *[1 mark]*.

Answers

11. The forwards reaction would be favoured *[1 mark]*. The right hand side contains fewer molecules of gas so the system would form more products in order to reduce the pressure (and so oppose the change) *[1 mark]*.

Test 17: Rate and Extent of Chemical Change
Pages 34–35

1. A *[1 mark]* 2. B *[1 mark]*
3. A *[1 mark]* 4. B *[1 mark]*
5. A *[1 mark]* 6. A *[1 mark]*
7. B *[1 mark]* 8. A *[1 mark]*
9. The forward and reverse reactions are occurring at exactly the same rate *[1 mark]*.
10. The volume of O_2 produced will stay the same *[1 mark]*. The total volume of O_2 produced is only affected by the initial amount of H_2O_2 *[1 mark]*.
11. Increasing the concentration of a solution increases the number of reactant particles in a given volume *[1 mark]* so will increase the frequency of collisions *[1 mark]*.
12. Rate of reaction = amount of product formed ÷ time = 10.2 ÷ 20 *[1 mark]* = 0.51 cm³/s *[1 mark]*.

Test 18: Organic Chemistry
Pages 36–37

1. B *[1 mark]* 2. B *[1 mark]*
3. C *[1 mark]* 4. B *[1 mark]*
5. C *[1 mark]* 6. A *[1 mark]*
7. B *[1 mark]* 8. B *[1 mark]*
9. carbon dioxide *[1 mark]*
10. They contain two fewer hydrogen atoms than the alkane with the same number of carbon atoms / a carbon-carbon double bond *[1 mark]*.
11. Addition polymerisation *[1 mark]*. Ethene molecules have C=C double bonds which can open up and join together to form a chain *[1 mark]*.
12. Name: propanoic acid *[2 marks — 1 mark for 'prop-', 1 mark for '-anoic acid']*
Other products formed: carbon dioxide and water *[1 mark]*.

Test 19: Organic Chemistry
Pages 38–39

1. C *[1 mark]* 2. A *[1 mark]*
3. B *[1 mark]* 4. C *[1 mark]*
5. B *[1 mark]* 6. B *[1 mark]*
7. A *[1 mark]* 8. A *[1 mark]*
9. $C_3H_8 + 5O_2 \rightarrow 3CO_2 + 4H_2O$
[2 marks — 1 mark for formulas, 1 mark for correct balancing]
10. Decane will have a higher boiling point *[1 mark]* because it has a longer hydrocarbon chain *[1 mark]*.
11. There is a temperature gradient in the column/the column gets cooler as you go up it *[1 mark]*. The fractions have different boiling points *[1 mark]* so they condense and drain out at different levels *[1 mark]*.

Test 20: Chemical Analysis
Pages 40–41

1. B *[1 mark]* 2. C *[1 mark]*
3. B *[1 mark]* 4. C *[1 mark]*
5. A *[1 mark]* 6. B *[1 mark]*
7. B *[1 mark]* 8. A *[1 mark]*
9. Silver chloride (AgCl) *[1 mark]*. White *[1 mark]*.
10. Any two of, e.g. they are very fast / they are very sensitive / they are very accurate *[1 mark each]*.
11. Iron(II) / Fe^{2+} *[1 mark]*
Bromide / Br^- *[1 mark]*.
12. Put damp litmus paper into the gas. Chlorine will turn the litmus paper white / bleach it *[1 mark]*.

Test 21: Chemical Analysis
Pages 42–43

1. C *[1 mark]* 2. A *[1 mark]*
3. B *[1 mark]* 4. A *[1 mark]*
5. B *[1 mark]* 6. C *[1 mark]*
7. A *[1 mark]* 8. C *[1 mark]*
9. Add an excess of sodium hydroxide to both solutions *[1 mark]*. The precipitate formed with the aluminium chloride solution will redissolve but the precipitate formed with the calcium chloride will remain *[1 mark]*.
10. Add barium chloride solution *[1 mark]*. 'white' *[1 mark]*.

11. $R_f = 3.2 \div 5$ *[1 mark]* = 0.64 *[1 mark]*
12. The water is impure *[1 mark]*.

Test 22: Chemistry of the Atmosphere
Pages 44–45

1. C *[1 mark]* 2. A *[1 mark]*
3. A *[1 mark]* 4. B *[1 mark]*
5. B *[1 mark]* 6. A *[1 mark]*
7. C *[1 mark]* 8. B *[1 mark]*
9. Any one action that a government could take: e.g. tax companies/individuals based on CO_2 emissions / invest in nuclear power/renewable energy resources that don't release CO_2 / cap emissions made by companies *[1 mark]*.
Any one reason their actions are limited: e.g. concern about impact on economic growth / alternative technologies still need development *[1 mark]*.
10. Green plants and algae decreased the carbon dioxide level and increased the oxygen level *[1 mark]* through photosynthesis *[1 mark]*.
11. Carbon dioxide *[1 mark]*.
E.g. methane / ammonia / water vapour / nitrogen *[1 mark]*.
From volcanic activity *[1 mark]*.

Test 23: Chemistry of the Atmosphere
Pages 46–47

1. A *[1 mark]* 2. C *[1 mark]*
3. A *[1 mark]* 4. B *[1 mark]*
5. A *[1 mark]* 6. A *[1 mark]*
7. B *[1 mark]* 8. C *[1 mark]*
9. Rising global temperatures could cause the ice caps to melt *[1 mark]*. This would cause a rise in sea level *[1 mark]*, leading to increased coastal flooding/erosion *[1 mark]*.
10. E.g. increased agriculture *[1 mark]*, as farm animals produce methane through their digestive processes *[1 mark]*. Creating waste *[1 mark]*, as methane is released by decomposition of waste *[1 mark]*.

Answers

Test 24: Using Resources
Pages 48–49
1. A *[1 mark]* 2. C *[1 mark]*
3. C *[1 mark]* 4. C *[1 mark]*
5. A *[1 mark]* 6. B *[1 mark]*
7. B *[1 mark]* 8. B *[1 mark]*
9. Any two of, e.g. mining ores damages the landscape. / Extracting the metal from the ore uses energy from burning fossil fuels, resulting in CO_2 emissions. / Waste is produced which must be disposed of. / Mining ores can destroy habitats *[2 marks]*
10. Any two of, e.g. bubbling chlorine gas through it / using ozone / using ultraviolet light *[2 marks]*
11. Increasing the temperature means the yield is reduced *[1 mark]*, but it also means the reaction takes place much quicker *[1 mark]*. 450 °C is a compromise between maximum yield and reaction rate *[1 mark]*.

Test 25: Using Resources
Pages 50–51
1. C *[1 mark]* 2. C *[1 mark]*
3. B *[1 mark]* 4. A *[1 mark]*
5. B *[1 mark]* 6. A *[1 mark]*
7. B *[1 mark]* 8. B *[1 mark]*
9. Calcium sulfate *[1 mark]* and calcium phosphate *[1 mark]*.
10. One material, a reinforcement, is embedded in another, a matrix/binder *[1 mark]*.
11. Getting the raw materials *[1 mark]*, manufacturing and packaging *[1 mark]*, using the product *[1 mark]*, disposal of the product *[1 mark]*.

Mixed Tests for Paper 2

Test 26: Paper 2 Mixed Topics
Pages 52–53
1. A *[1 mark]* 2. B *[1 mark]*
3. B *[1 mark]* 4. B *[1 mark]*
5. C *[1 mark]* 6. A *[1 mark]*
7. B *[1 mark]* 8. C *[1 mark]*
9. Name: methanol *[1 mark]*. Uses: as a solvent *[1 mark]* and a fuel *[1 mark]*.
10. A pure substance will leave a single spot on the chromatography paper *[1 mark]*. An impure substance will leave multiple spots *[1 mark]*.
11. Le Chatelier's principle states that if you change the conditions of a reversible reaction at equilibrium *[1 mark]*, the system will try to counteract that change *[1 mark]*.

Test 27: Paper 2 Mixed Topics
Pages 54–55
1. A *[1 mark]* 2. A *[1 mark]*
3. B *[1 mark]* 4. B *[1 mark]*
5. C *[1 mark]* 6. C *[1 mark]*
7. A *[1 mark]* 8. B *[1 mark]*
9. E.g. borosilicate glass melts at a higher temperature than soda-lime glass *[1 mark]*.
10. Line 2 *[1 mark]*. Line 2 has a lower initial rise in energy than line 1, showing a lower activation energy *[1 mark]*.
11. Greenhouse gases absorb long wavelength radiation *[1 mark]* reflected off the Earth *[1 mark]*. They then re-radiate it in all directions, including back to the surface of the Earth *[1 mark]*. Long wavelength radiation is thermal radiation so this results in warming of the Earth *[1 mark]*.

Test 28: Paper 2 Mixed Topics
Pages 56–57
1. B *[1 mark]* 2. A *[1 mark]*
3. A *[1 mark]* 4. A *[1 mark]*
5. B *[1 mark]* 6. A *[1 mark]*
7. C *[1 mark]* 8. B *[1 mark]*
9. Put one iron nail in a test tube of water which has been boiled to remove air and has oil on the top to stop air getting in *[1 mark]*. Put a second nail in a test tube with just air (use calcium chloride to absorb any water in the air) *[1 mark]*. Put a third nail in a test tube with water and air *[1 mark]*. Compare the nails after a few days *[1 mark]*.
10. A selective life cycle assessment only shows some environmental impacts of a product *[1 mark]*. Companies may select impacts in a biased way to support their own products or claims *[1 mark]*.
11. Around 37 °C *[1 mark]*.

Test 29: Paper 2 Mixed Topics
Pages 58–59
1. B *[1 mark]* 2. B *[1 mark]*
3. B *[1 mark]* 4. B *[1 mark]*
5. A *[1 mark]* 6. C *[1 mark]*
7. B *[1 mark]* 8. B *[1 mark]*
9. Alloy: bronze *[1 mark]*
   Use: making, e.g. medals/ornaments/statues *[1 mark]*
10. $2CH_3OH + 3O_2 \rightarrow 2CO_2 + 4H_2O$
    [1 mark for H_2O, 1 mark for correct balancing]
11. It will increase the rate of the reaction *[1 mark]* because the surface area of the solid is increased *[1 mark]*, meaning more frequent collisions between reactants *[1 mark]*.

Test 30: Paper 2 Mixed Topics
Pages 60–61
1. B *[1 mark]* 2. B *[1 mark]*
3. C *[1 mark]* 4. C *[1 mark]*
5. B *[1 mark]* 6. B *[1 mark]*
7. C *[1 mark]* 8. A *[1 mark]*
9. There are fewer molecules of gas products than gas reactants *[1 mark]*, so increasing the pressure moves the position of equilibrium towards the products, meaning a higher yield *[1 mark]*. Increased pressure also increases the frequency of collisions and therefore the rate of reaction *[1 mark]*.
10. Part 1: effluent *[1 mark]*
    Process used to treat it: aerobic digestion *[1 mark]*
    Part 2: sludge *[1 mark]*
    Process used to treat it: anaerobic digestion *[1 mark]*.